Panoramic Journey Through

KWAZULU-NATAL

Panoramic Journey Through

KWAZULU-NATAL

SHAEN ADEY

First published in 2000 by Struik Publishers (Pty) Ltd
(a member of Struik New Holland Publishing (Pty) Ltd)

London • Cape Town • Sydney • Auckland

24 Nutford Place
London W1H 6DQ
United Kingdom

14 Aquatic Drive
Frenchs Forest
NSW 2086, Australia

80 McKenzie Street
Cape Town 8001
South Africa

218 Lake Road
Northcote, Auckland
New Zealand

10 9 8 7 6 5 4 3 2 1

DESIGNER Tracey Mackenzie
DESIGN MANAGER Janice Evans
EDITOR Lesley Hay-Whitton
MANAGING EDITOR Annlerie van Rooyen
PICTURE RESEARCHER Carmen Watts
FRENCH TRANSLATOR Jean-Paul Houssière
GERMAN TRANSLATOR Friedel Herrmann

ISBN 1 86872 471 9

Reproduction by Disc Express Cape (Pty) Ltd
Printed and bound by Times Offset (M) Sdn Bhd

ENDPAPERS *Fishermen at Bhanga Nek, north of Sodwana Bay.*
PAGE 1 *Durban's Esplanade, with Sea World in the foreground.*
PAGES 2 AND 3 *Glengary farm, a trout-fishing area in the Kamberg, Drakensberg.*
THIS PAGE *Curios for sale at Shaka's Kraal, a Zulu cultural village.*

INTRODUCTION

KwaZulu-Natal, rich in natural beauty, lists among its numerous game and nature reserves the Hluhluwe-Umfolozi Park and the Greater St Lucia Wetland Park, a wetland of international significance. The province is home to diverse cultural groups, among them the Zulu and Indian peoples. Outdoor enthusiasts enjoy diving, surfing and bathing in the warm Indian Ocean, and the spectacular Drakensberg range offers horseback riding and hiking.

INTRODUCTION

Le KwaZulu-Natal, province d'une grande beauté, possède le Hluhluwe-Umfolozi Park, renommé pour sa faune, et le St Lucia Wetland Park, une zone marécageuse d'importance internationale sur le plan écologique. La région compte une grande diversité de groupes culturels, parmi lesquels on trouve les Zoulous et les Indiens. Les sportifs et amateurs de plein air pourront s'adonner à la plongée, le surf et la nage dans les eaux chaudes de l'océan Indien, et dans le splendide Drakensberg, à l'équitation et aux randonnées.

EINFÜHRUNG

KwaZulu-Natal ist reich an kultureller Vielfalt und Naturschönheit und hat zahlreiche Wildreservate und Naturschutzgebiete, wie das Hluhluwe-Umfolozi Wildreservat und den Greater St. Lucia Wetlandpark, ein Sumpfgebiet von internationaler Bedeutung. Das warme Wasser des Indischen Ozeans verlockt zum Tauchen, Schwimmen und Wellenreiten, und Naturliebhaber genießen die herrliche Landschaft der Drakensberge zum Reiten und Wandern. Die Völkergruppen der Zulus und Inder geben der Region ihre besondere Prägung.

LEFT *A mother and calf black rhino. In the 1960s Operation Rhino, launched in the Hluhluwe-Umfolozi Park (then two separate reserves), helped rescue the rhino from extinction.*
A GAUCHE *Un rhinocéros noir femelle et son petit, fruit de l'Opération rhino mise en action durant les années '60, à Hluhluwe-Umfolozi Park (à cette époque, 2 réserves distinctes).*
LINKS *Die Spitzmaulnashornkuh und ihr Kalb bezeugen, wie erfolgreich das Schutzprojekt war, das in den sechziger Jahren in Hluhluwe-Umfolozi (derzeitig noch getrennte Wildreservate) anlief.*

ABOVE *A boardsailor off Durban's Vetche's Beach. Boardsailing is one of the many watersport activities for the outdoor enthusiast along KwaZulu-Natal's long golden coastline.*
CI-DESSUS *Un véliplanchiste au large de Vetche's Beach, à Durban. La planche à voile est un des nombreux sports pratiqués le long du magnifique littoral du KwaZulu-Natal.*
OBEN *Windsegler vor Vetches Beach bei Durban. Die langen goldenen Strände an der Küste von KwaZulu-Natal sind ein Paradies für Wassersportenthusiasten.*

RIGHT *North Beach, a little way up Durban's coast, attracts swimmers, surfers and sunbathers.*
A DROITE *North Beach, un Eden où se retrouvent les baigneurs, surfeurs et amateurs de bronzage.*
RECHTS *North Beach, etwas nördlich gelegen, lockt Sonnenanbeter, Badende und Wellenreiter.*

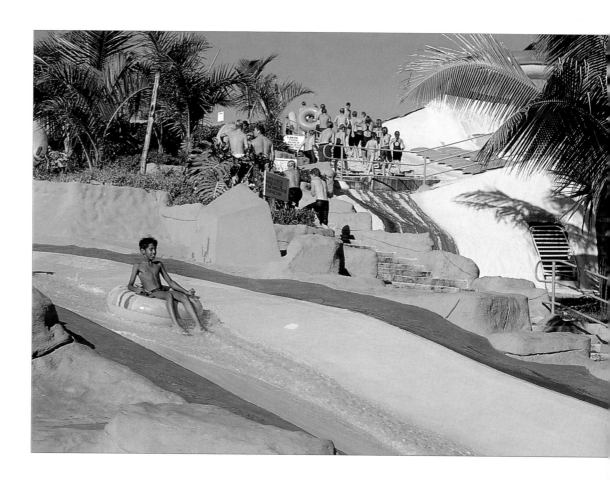

THIS PAGE *Paddling pools* (LEFT) *and
Water World* (ABOVE and RIGHT) *are part
of Durban's Golden Mile, stretching from
the Point to the Umgeni River mouth.*
CETTE PAGE *Le 'Golden Mile' de Durban
s'étend du 'Point' jusqu'à l'embouchure
de l'Umgeni. On y trouve de nombreuses
attractions aquatiques.*
DIESE SEITE *Die Planschbecken* (LINKS)
und Water World (OBEN UND RECHTS) *auf
Durbans 'Goldener Meile', die vom 'Point'
bis zur Mündung des Umgeni reicht.*

LEFT *Durban's Victoria Embankment provides mooring for small crafts such as these yachts.*
À GAUCHE *Le 'Victoria Embankment' de Durban, où sont amarrés les yachts et autres bateaux de plaisance.*
LINKS *Durbans Victoriabecken bietet Anlegeplätze für Jachten und andere Boote.*

BELOW *Dolphins, as well as penguins and seals, are among the aquatic animals that may be seen at Sea World.*
CI-DESSOUS *On trouvera de nombreux animaux à 'Sea World', entre eux des dauphins, des pingouins et des phoques.*
UNTEN *Delphine, Pinguine, Robben und andere Meerestiere kann man in Sea World aus der Nähe betrachten.*

The Victoria Street Indian market is an ideal place to buy fragrant spices.
CI-DESSUS *Le marché de Victoria Street, où l'on trouve un ample choix d'épices aromatiques.*
OBEN *Auf dem Markt in der Victoria Street gibt es ein großes Angebot duftender Gewürze.*

RIGHT *Colourfully dressed ricksha drivers transport tourists along Durban's beachfront.*
A DROITE *Les conducteurs de ricksha, vêtus d'ornements multicolores, attendent les touristes.*
RECHTS *Malerisch geschmückte Rickschafahrer befördern Touristen an der Strandpromenade.*

ABOVE *Brightly coloured saris may be purchased at Durban's Indian Market.*

CI-DESSUS *Le marché Indien de Durban, où l'on trouvera de splendides saris aux couleurs vives.*

OBEN *Der Indermarkt in Durban bietet eine große Auswahl an farbenfreudigen Saris.*

RIGHT *Zulu beadwork, pots and baskets are sold along the Esplanade.*

A DROITE *Des ornements, pots et paniers, sont en vente à l'Esplanade.*

RECHTS *An der Esplanade werden Perlenarbeiten, Körbe und Töpfe der Zulus angeboten.*

OPPOSITE *The late-Victorian City Hall between West and Smith streets.*

CI-CONTRE *L'hôtel de ville, en style fin victorien, situé entre les rues West et Smith.*

LINKE SEITE *Das Rathaus im viktorianischen Baustil liegt zwischen Weststraße und Smithstraße.*

RIGHT AND BELOW *Durban has many beautiful mosques and Muslim shrines, testimony to the city's large Islamic population.*

A DROITE ET CI-DESSOUS *Durban possède de belles mosquées et autres sanctuaires musulmans, témoignant de la nombreuse population islamique.*

RECHTS UND UNTEN *Durban hat viele schöne Moscheen und islamitische Gedenkstätten, die Zeugnis ablegen von dem großen Anteil Muslimen in der Bevölkerung.*

BELOW *A colourful inhabitant of the Umgeni Bird Park.*

CI-DESSOUS *Un original citoyen du Umgeni Bird Park.*

UNTEN *Ein farbenfreudiger Bewohner des Vogelparks bei Umgeni.*

RIGHT *The picturesque Japanese Gardens, situated in Durban North.*

A DROITE *Les pittoresques Jardins Japonais, à Durban North.*

RECHTS *Die zauberhaften japanischen Gärten im Norden von Durban.*

LEFT AND BELOW *Oribi Gorge, a 24-km-long canyon some 20 km inland from Port Shepstone on the South Coast, is in a nature reserve that is home to about 40 mammal species.*

À GAUCHE ET CI-DESSOUS *Oribi Gorge est un canyon de 24 km, situé dans une réserve naturelle, à l'intérieur des terres, à quelque 20km de Port Shepstone, sur la South Coast. La réserve est l'habitat d'une quarantaine d'espèces de mammifères.*

LINKS UND UNTEN *Oribi Gorge, eine 24km lange Felsschlucht, etwa 20km landeinwärts von Port Shepstone gelegen, ist ein Naturschutzgebiet, wo etwa 40 verschiedene Säugetierarten leben.*

ABOVE *Fields of sugar cane near Pennington along the South Coast.*
CI-DESSUS *Canne à sucre, près de Pennington, sur la South Coast.*
OBEN *Zuckerrohrfelder bei Pennington an der Südküste.*

OPPOSITE *Margate, one of the South Coast's more popular resorts.*
CI-CONTRE *Margate, un centre de villégiature sur la South Coast.*
GEGENÜBER *Margate, eines der beliebten Ferienorte an der Südküste.*

24

THIS PAGE *Pietermaritzburg lies to the north-west of Durban. Its Victorian City Hall* (RIGHT) *is testimony to its colonial past, as are statues of Mahatma Gandhi* (BELOW LEFT) *and of Queen Victoria* (BELOW RIGHT).

CETTE PAGE *Pietermaritzburg, au nord-ouest de Durban. Son Hôtel de Ville* (À DROITE) *en style victorien, ainsi que ses statues du mahatma Gandhi* (CI-DESSOUS, À GAUCHE) *et de la reine Victoria* (CI-DESSOUS, À DROITE), *attestent de son passé colonial.*

DIESE SEITE *Pietermaritzburg liegt nordwestlich von Durban. Das Rathaus im viktorianischen Baustil* (RECHTS) *und die Statuen von Mahatma Gandhi* (UNTEN LINKS) *und Königin Viktoria* (UNTEN RECHTS) *legen alle Zeugnis ab von der Geschichte.*

ABOVE   *Valley of a Thousand Hills stretches 65 km from 'Natal Table Mountain' near Pietermaritzburg to the Indian Ocean in the east.*
CI-DESSUS   *La 'Vallée aux mille collines' s'étend de la 'Montagne de la Table' du Natal, près de Pietermaritzburg, à l'océan Indien.*
OBEN   *Das Tal der tausend Hügel erstreckt sich über 65km vom 'Tafelberg Natals' bei Pietermaritzburg ostwärts bis zum Indischen Ozean.*

OPPOSITE   *The glorious Howick Falls, which plunge some 95 m into the Umgeni River, in the picturesque KwaZulu-Natal Midlands.*
CI-CONTRE   *Les splendides Howick Falls, dans le pittoresque KwaZulu-Natal Midlands, se précipitent dans l'Umgeni, d'une hauteur de 95m.*
GEGENÜBER   *Die eindrucksvollen Howickfälle in den malerischen KwaZulu-Natal Midlands stürzen über 95m herab in den Umgenifluß.*

PREVIOUS PAGES *Rawdons Hotel, a delightful place to break a scenic journey through the KwaZulu-Natal Midlands.*

PAGES PRÉCÉDENTES *Le Rawdons Hotel est un endroit charmant où s'attarder, en explorant les splendides Midlands.*

VORIGE SEITEN *Rawdons Hotel ist eine besonders einladende Zwischenstation auf der Reise durch die schönen Midlands.*

THIS PAGE *In 1985 a group of locals formed the 'Midlands Meander', an arts and crafts route from Mooi River to Hilton. Among the route's attractions are a restored settlers' house* (OPPOSITE), *and crafts such as leatherwork* (TOP RIGHT) *and weaving* (BOTTOM RIGHT).

CETTE PAGE *En 1985, une association de résidents de la région créa le 'Midlands Meander' (flâner dans les Midlands), un itinéraire menant de Mooi River à Hilton, qui offre de nombreuses attractions artisanales sur son parcours. On y trouvera la maison restaurée d'un ancien pionnier* (CI-CONTRE), *des produits d'artisanat en cuir* (CI-DESSUS À DROITE) *et de tissage* (CI-DESSOUS, À DROITE).

DIESE SEITE *Eine Gruppe Ortsansässiger gründete 1985 'Midlands Meander', eine Straße für Kunstgewerbe von Mooi River bis Hilton. Ein rekonstruiertes Siedlerhaus* (LINKS) *ist eine der Attraktionen und Handarbeiten wie Lederwaren* (RECHTS OBEN) *und Webarbeiten* (RECHTS UNTEN) *werden zum Verkauf angeboten.*

THIS PAGE *During the 19th century many battles were fought between the Zulu and the British. The Midlands Battlefield Route commemorates fallen heroes and battles such as Isandlwana (OPPOSITE), eMgungundlovu (ABOVE) and Fugitives' Drift (RIGHT).*
CETTE PAGE *Isandlwana (CI-CONTRE), eMgungudlovu (CI-DESSUS) et Fugitives' Drift (À DROITE) sont situés sur un itinéraire établi à la mémoire des héros tombés dans les engagements entre Zoulous et Britanniques au 19ième siècle.*
DIESE SEITE *Im 19. Jahrhundert gab es viele Kämpfe zwischen Zulus und Briten. Die 'Midlands Battlefield Route' gedenkt der Gefallenen und der Schlachten wie Isandlwana (LINKS) eMgundgundlovu (OBEN) und Fugutives' Drift (RECHTS).*

FOLLOWING PAGES *A view towards Garden Castle in the southern Drakensberg.*
PAGES SUIVANTES *Le panorama de Garden Castle dans le Drankensberg méridional.*
UMSEITIG *Blick auf Garden Castle in den südlichen Drakensbergen.*

PREVIOUS PAGES   *The Drakensberg Amphitheatre provides a dramatic backdrop to Tendele Camp.*
PAGES PRÉCÉDENTES   *Le Tendele Camp, avec, à l'arrière-plan, le 'Drakensberg Amphithéâtre.'*
VORIGE SEITE   *Das Amphitheater der Drakensberge ist eine Kulisse für das Tendele Rastlager.*

BELOW   *The bearded vulture (lammergeier) is found in isolated groups in the Drakensberg.*
CI-DESSOUS   *Le 'vautour barbu' se trouve en petits groupes isolés, par delà le Drakensberg.*
UNTEN   *Der Bartgeier kommt in den Drakensbergen in vereinzelten Gruppen vor.*

RIGHT   *Hikers enjoy the spectacular view from the top of the Amphitheatre.*
A DROITE   *Deux randonneurs admirent le panorama au sommet de l'Amphithéâtre.*
RECHTS   *Wanderer genießen den wunderbaren Ausblick vom Gipfel des Amphitheaters.*

FOLLOWING PAGES   *One of the scenic walks in the Royal Natal National Park leads to the Cascades.*
PAGES SUIVANTES   *'Cascades Walk', un des circuits touristiques du Royal Natal National Park.*
UMSEITIG   *Cascades Walk, einer der malerischen Wanderwege im Royal Natal Nationalpark.*

40

OPPOSITE *Walkers on a footpath that leads to the magnificent Tugela Gorge in the Royal Natal National Park.*

CI-CONTRE *Des randonneurs en route vers l'extraordinaire Tugela Gorge, dans le Royal Natal National Park.*

GEGENÜBER *Wanderer auf einem Pfad zur imposanten Tugelaschlucht im Royal Natal Nationalpark.*

ABOVE *A hiker crossing a stream on the 22-km (return) walk to the Tugela Gorge.*

CI-DESSUS *Une randonneuse traverse un torrent, en route vers la Tugela Gorge. Le trajet aller-retour est long de 22km.*

OBEN *Ein Wanderer überquert einen Bach auf der 22km langen Strecke zur Tugelaschlucht.*

LEFT *The start of the 948-m-high Tugela Falls, the second highest in the world.*
A GAUCHE *Le début des Tugela Falls, longues de 948m, les deuxièmes au monde en hauteur.*
LINKS *Der Beginn der Tugelafälle, die mit 948m die zweithöchsten der Welt sind.*

BELOW *The diverse flora in the Royal Natal National Park includes*
Hesperantha coccinea (LEFT) *and* Clematis brachiata (RIGHT).
CI-DESSOUS *Deux des variétés trouvées dans le Royal Natal*
National Park, Hesperantha coccinea (À GAUCHE) *et* Clematis
brachiata (À DROITE).
UNTEN *Die* Hesperantha coccinea (LINKS) *und die* Clematis brachiata
(RECHTS) *gehören zur vielfältigen Flora im Royal Natal Nationalpark.*

OPPOSITE *The path to the Tugela Gorge leads through lush vegetation.*
CI-CONTRE *Le chemin vers la gorge traverse une végétation luxuriante.*
GEGENÜBER *Der Pfad in die Schlucht führt durch üppige Vegetation.*

FOLLOWING PAGES *Dawn breaks over snow-covered mountains.*
PAGES SUIVANTES *Le jour se lève sur les sommets enneigés.*
UMSEITIG *Die Morgensonne tastet sich über die schneebedeckten Berge.*

LEFT *The escarpment as seen in the early morning from Giant's Castle Nature Reserve.*

A GAUCHE *L'escarpement de 'Giant's Castle Reserve' (Réserve naturelle du château du géant) vu au petit matin.*

LINKS *Blick auf den Steilabbruch im Morgenlicht vom Giant's Castle Naturschutzgebiet.*

BELOW *A black eagle taking off from the 'restaurant' at the Giant's Castle hide.*

CI-DESSOUS *Un aigle noir prend son envol au 'Giant's Castle'.*

UNTEN *Ein Kaffernadler hebt ab von der Futterstelle für Geier bei Giant's Castle.*

THIS PAGE *A popular pastime of the 'Berg is trout fishing, here at Lake Navarone* (BELOW) *and in the Kamberg Nature Reserve* (RIGHT).

CETTE PAGE *La pêche à la truite est un passe temps populaire au Drakensberg. Ici, au lac Navarone* (CI-DESSOUS), *et à Kamberg Nature Reserve* (À DROITE).

DIESE SEITE *Forellenangeln ist eine beliebte Freizeitgestaltung in den Drakensbergen, wie hier am Navaronesee* (UNTEN) *und im Kamberg Naturschutzgebiet* (RECHTS).

THIS PAGE *Snow-capped mountains near the Kamberg* (OPPOSITE). *The Kamberg region boasts excellent examples of San rock art* (BELOW).

CETTE PAGE *Sommets sous la neige, près de Kamberg* (CI-CONTRE). *Le Kamberg s'enorgueillit de peintures rupestres San* (CI-DESSOUS).

DIESE SEITE *Schneebedeckte Berggipfel in der Nähe des Kamberg* (GEGENÜBER). *Im Kamberg findet man auch Felsmalereien der Drakensberg San* (UNTEN).

FOLLOWING PAGES *The rolling landscape of rural KwaZulu-Natal is dotted with Zulu homes, here at Injasuti.*

PAGES SUIVANTES *La campagne du KwaZulu-Natal est parsemées de huttes zouloues. Cette photo montre Injasuti.*

UMSEITIG *Das Landesinnere von KwaZulu-Natal hat ein ländliches Gepräge mit verstreuten Heimstätten der Zulu, wie hier in Injasuti.*

OPPOSITE *Injasuti Camp nestles in a picturesque valley.*

CI-CONTRE *Injasuti Camp, blotti dans une vallée pittoresque.*

GEGENÜBER *Das Rastlager von Injasuti nestelt in einem malerischen Tal.*

ABOVE *A hiker takes a rest on the footpath above Injasuti Camp.*

CI-DESSUS *Un randonneur sur le sentier surplombant Injasuti Camp.*

OBEN *Ein Wanderer ruht sich aus oberhalb des Injasuti Rastlagers.*

THIS PAGE *Zulu basket makers sell their wares in the Cathedral Peak area* (BELOW).
Cathedral Peak is a favourite spot for climbing in the 'Berg (RIGHT).

CETTE PAGE *Des vanniers Zoulous vendent leur ouvrage dans la région de Cathedral
Peak* (CI-DESSOUS). *Cathedral Peak est un des endroits favoris du Drakensberg pour
l'escalade* (À DROITE).

DIESE SEITE *Korbwaren der Zulus werden in der Umgebung von Cathedral Peak
angeboten* (UNTEN). *Cathedral Peak ist eine von Bergsteigern sehr beliebte Gegend in
den Drakensbergen* (RECHTS).

THIS PAGE *At Shaka's Kraal, the Zulu people follow a traditional lifestyle, the girls wearing colourful beaded skirts* (LEFT), *the young Zulu men participating in stick-fighting and dancing* (BELOW). *A warrior outside a beehive dwelling with thatched roof* (OPPOSITE).

CETTE PAGE *Shaka's Kraal. Des jeunes guerriers Zoulous attendent de commencer leur danse* (CI-DESSOUS). *Les jeunes filles Zouloues portent des jupes de perles aux couleurs vives* (À GAUCHE). *Une hutte traditionnelle au toit de chaume, en forme de ruche* (CI-CONTRE).

DIESE SEITE *Eine Gruppe junger Zulus wartet auf den Anfang der Tänze in Shaka's Kraal* (UNTEN). *Zulumädchen tragen farbenfreudige Perlenröcke* (LINKS). *Traditionelle Rundhütte mit Strohdach* (GEGENÜBER).

RIGHT *A Zulu maiden at Dumazulu*
Cultural Village, south of the village
of Hluhluwe in northern KwaZulu-Natal.
In traditional society unmarried girls go
bare-breasted and -headed.
A DROITE *Une jeune Zouloue du village*
culturel de Dumazulu, au sud de
Hluhluwe, dans le nord du KwaZulu-
Natal. Il est de tradition chez les
Zoulous, que les filles non mariées ne
se couvrent ni la tête, ni la poitrine.
RECHTS *Zulumädchen in Dumazulu,*
einem Museumsdorf südlich von
Hluhluwe im nördlichen KwaZulu-Natal.
Stammesbräuchen entsprechend haben
unverheiratete Mädchen Kopf und
Brust unbedeckt.

66

LEFT *A sangoma (traditional healer) at Hluhluwe Cultural Village.*
A GAUCHE *Un sangoma (féticheur) au village culturel de Hluhluwe.*
LINKS *Ein Sangoma (Heilkundiger) im Museumsdorf bei Hluhluwe.*

BELOW *A brightly decorated shop in Hluhluwe village.*
CI-DESSOUS *Une échoppe à la façade décorée de couleurs vives.*
UNTEN *Bunt bemalter Laden im Museumsdorf bei Hluhluwe.*

OPPOSITE *The Black Umfolozi River, Hluhluwe-Umfolozi Park.*
CI-CONTRE *La rivière Black Umfolozi, au Hluhluwe-Umfolozi Park.*
GEGENÜBER *Der Schwarze Umfolozi-Fluß im Wildreservat.*

LEFT *A waterbuck in the Umfolozi section of the Hluhluwe-Umfolozi Park.*
A GAUCHE *Une antilope au Hluhluwe-Umfolozi Park.*
LINKS *Ein Wasserbock im Umfolozi-Teil des Wildreservats.*

BELOW *White rhino in the Hluhluwe section. The park is renowned for Operation Rhino, which helped saved the rhino from extinction.*
CI-DESSOUS *Un rhinocéros blanc dans la section de Hluhluwe. Le parc est renommé pour son 'Opération rhino' qui contribua à préserver l'espèce.*
UNTEN *Breitmaulnashörner im Hluhluwe-Teil des Wildreservats. Das 'Operation Rhino'-Projekt hat viel zum Erhalt der Nashörner beigetragen.*

THIS PAGE *Accommodation in the Hluhluwe section of the Hluhluwe-Umfolozi Park includes Hilltop Camp with its stunning views* (LEFT) *and Muntulu Bush Lodge* (ABOVE).

CETTE PAGE *Les gîtes dans la section de Hluhluwe du Hluhluwe-Umfolozi Park, comprennent Hilltop Camp, avec ses vues remarquables* (À GAUCHE), *et Muntulu Bush Lodge* (CI-DESSUS).

DIESE SEITE *Im Hluhluwe-Teil des Hluhluwe-Umfolozi Wildreservats gibt es Unterkunfts-möglichkeiten im Hilltop Rastlager mit seinem atemberaubenden Ausblick* (LINKS) *und in der Muntulu Bush Lodge* (OBEN).

THIS PAGE *The abundant game that may be encountered in the Umfolozi section of the Hluhluwe-Umfolozi Park includes lion* (RIGHT), *cheetah* (BELOW) *and giraffe* (OPPOSITE).

CETTE PAGE *La section Umfolozi du Hluhluwe-Umfolozi Park abonde en animaux sauvages. On y verra des lions* (À DROITE), *des guépards* (CI-DESSOUS) *et des girafes* (CI-CONTRE, À DROITE).

DIESE SEITE *Zu den vielen Wildarten, denen man im Umfolozi-Teil des Hluhluwe-Umfolozi Wildreservats begegnet, zählen Löwen* (RECHTS), *Geparden* (UNTEN) *und Giraffen* (GEGENÜBER).

THIS PAGE *Guided hiking trails are conducted in Hluhluwe-Umfolozi: hikers crossing the White Umfolozi River* (LEFT) *and examining a rhino midden in the Umfolozi section* (ABOVE). CETTE PAGE *A Hluhluwe-Umfolozi, les randonneurs trouveront des guides qui les mèneront en brousse; ici, un groupe traverse la White Umfolozi* (À GAUCHE). *Examinant du crottin de rhinocéros dans la section d'Umfolozi* (CI-DESSUS). DIESE SEITE *Im Hluhluwe-Umfolozi Wildreservat gibt es geführte Wanderungen. Hier beim Überqueren des Weißen Umfolozi* (LINKS) *und beim Betrachten von Nashornlosung* (OBEN).

BELOW *A mountain zebra in Itala Game Reserve, northern KwaZulu-Natal.*

CI-DESSOUS *Un zèbre de montagne, à Itala Game Reserve, dans le nord du KwaZulu-Natal.*

UNTEN *Bergzebra im Itala Wildreservat im nördlichen KwaZulu-Natal.*

RIGHT *Visitors on a game drive in Itala watching a zebra and rhino mother and calf.*

A DROITE *Des visiteurs observent un zèbre ainsi qu'un rhinocéros femelle et son petit à Itala Game Reserve.*

RECHTS *Auf einer Pirschfahrt in Itala beobachten Besucher ein Zebra und eine Nashornmutter mit Kalb.*

THIS PAGE *Four self-guided nature trails may be undertaken from Itala's Ntshondwe Camp* (LEFT), *seen here from the hills above the camp. The camp's attractive reception centre* (ABOVE).
CETTE PAGE *Ntshondwe Camp, à Itala, vu des collines le surplombant. Ce camp est le point de départ de quatre pistes que les visiteurs peuvent explorer sans guide* (À GAUCHE). *Le charmant centre d'accueil* (CI-DESSUS).
DIESE SEITE *Vom Ntshondwe Rastlager in Itala – hier von den umliegenden Hügeln aus gesehen – kann man vier Wanderungen eigenständig unternehmen* (LINKS). *Der einlandende Empfang des Rastlagers* (OBEN).

BELOW *A Nile crocodile carrying her baby at the Crocodile Centre, north of St Lucia village.*
CI-DESSOUS *Au Crocodile Centre, au nord du village St Lucia, un crocodile transporte son petit.*
UNTEN *Ein Nilkrokodil trägt ihr Junges im Crocodile Centre, nördlich vom Dorf St. Lucia.*

RIGHT *Dawn over Fanie's Island on Lake St Lucia in the Greater St Lucia Wetland Park.*
A DROITE *Le jour se lève sur Fanie's Island, dans le Greater St Lucia Wetland Park.*
RECHTS *Sonnenaufgang über Fanie's Island auf dem St. Lucia See.*

FOLLOWING PAGES *Walking across the dunes at Cape Vidal, Greater St Lucia Wetland Park.*
PAGES SUIVANTES *En promenade dans les dunes de Cape Vidal, Greater St Lucia Wetland Park.*
UMSEITIG *Dünenwanderung bei Cape Vidal im Greater St. Lucia Wetlandpark.*

80

OPPOSITE *Fishermen near the mouth of St Lucia estuary.*

CI-CONTRE *Des pêcheurs près de l'embouchure de l'estuaire de St Lucia.*

GEGENÜBER *Angler an der Mündung des Ästuars von St. Lucia.*

BELOW *One of the cruise boats that operate on Lake St Lucia.*

CI-DESSOUS *Un des bateaux de plaisance qui opèrent sur Lake St Lucia.*

UNTEN *Eines der Schiffe, die Kreuzfahrten auf dem St. Lucia See anbieten.*

THIS PAGE *A group of divers about to explore the underwater marvels of the Indian Ocean off Sodwana Bay* (BELOW). *A diver has a close encounter with a dusky rubberlip* (Plectorhinchus chubbi) *on the brilliantly coloured coral reefs off Sodwana Bay* (RIGHT).
CETTE PAGE *A Sodwana Bay, un groupe de plongeurs se prépare à explorer les merveilles submergées de l'océan Indien* (CI-DESSOUS). *Sur un fond de coraux aux couleurs éclatantes, au large de Sodwana Bay, un plongeur nage en compagnie d'un résident de l'endroit* (À DROITE).
DIESE SEITE *Eine Gruppe Taucher steht bereit, die Wunderwelt des Meeres im Indischen Ozean bei Sodwana Bay zu erkunden* (UNTEN). *Ein Taucher vergnügt sich unter den Fischen in den bunten Korallenriffen vor Sodwana Bay* (RECHTS).

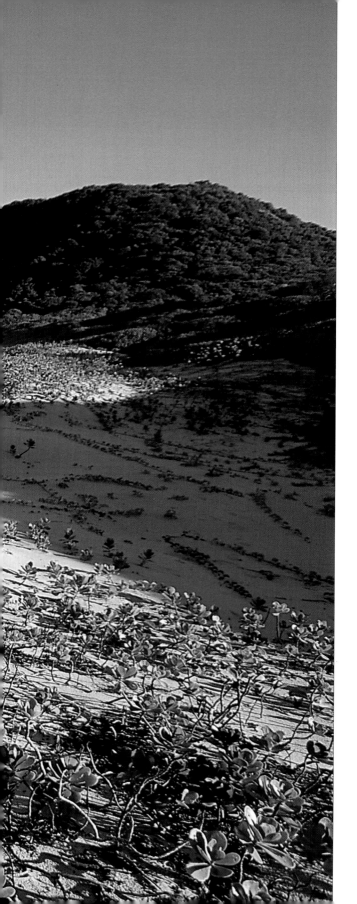

THIS PAGE *Dune vegetation at Bhanga Nek, north of Sodwana Bay* (LEFT). *During the summer months turtle tours are conducted along the northern KwaZulu-Natal coast, allowing close-up viewing of the nesting activities of this protected animal* (ABOVE and TOP).

CETTE PAGE *Végétation sur les dunes de Bhanga Nek, au nord de Sodwana Bay* (À GAUCHE). *En été, le littoral du nord du KwaZulu-Natal est un site de nidification des tortues de mer* (CI-DESSUS, et EN HAUT).

DIESE SEITE *Dünenvegetation bei Bhanga Nek, nördlich von Sodwana Bay* (LINKS). *An der Nordküste von KwaZulu-Natal gibt es im Sommer Führungen zu den Gelegen der Meeresschildkröten* (OBEN und GANZ OBEN).

BELOW *Mkuzi Game Reserve's tented camps are comfortable accommodation options.*

CI-DESSOUS *Tout le confort dans un des villages de toile à Mkuzi Game Reserve.*

UNTEN *Die Zeltlager im Mkuzi Wildreservat bieten komfortable Unterkünfte.*

BOTTOM *A group of hippo in Nsumu Pan, Mkuzi Game Reserve.*

EN BAS *Une troupe d'hippopotames à Nsumu Pan, dans Mkuzi Game Reserve.*

GANZ UNTEN *Flußpferde in der Nsumu-Pfanne im Mkuzi Wildreservat.*

RIGHT *Fever trees on Nsumu Pan, whose waters supply food for a wide variety of waterbirds.*

A DROITE *Arbres à fièvre à Nsumu Pan, où s'alimentent une grande variété d'oiseaux aquatiques.*

RECHTS *Fieberbäume an der Nsumu-Pfanne, die eine große Vielzahl Wasservögel ernährt.*

OPPOSITE *Fish traps, Kosi Bay estuary, near the Mozambican border.*

CI-CONTRE *Pièges à poisson dans l'estuaire de Kosi Bay.*

UMSEITIG *Fischfallen im Kosi Bay Ästuar an der Mosambikgrenze.*

ABOVE *A Kosi Bay fisherman spears his catch in the fish trap.*

CI-DESSUS *Un pêcheur de Kosi Bay harponne sa prise dans le piège.*

OBEN *Ein Fischer von Kosi Bay spießt seinen Fang in den Fischfallen auf.*

ABOVE *The scene from the viewing tower in Ndumo Game Reserve.*
CI-DESSUS *La vue de la tour d'observation de Ndumo Game Reserve.*
OBEN *Blick vom Aussichtsturm im Ndumo Wildreservat.*

OPPOSITE *A game drive among the fever trees of Nyamithi Pan, Ndumo.*
CI-CONTRE *Visiteurs observant les animaux sauvages à Ndumo.*
GEGENÜBER *Pirschfahrt durch die Fieberbäume der Nyamithi-Pfanne.*

FOLLOWING PAGE *Hiking among the fig forest of Shokwe Pan is one of the many attractions of Ndumo Game Reserve.*
PAGE SUIVANTE *Un des nombreux charmes de Ndumo: une randonnée dans la forêt de figuiers.*
UMSEITIG *Besucher genießen eine Wanderung durch den Feigenwald an der Shokwe-Pfanne, eine der vielen Attraktionen, die das Ndumo Wildreservat zu bieten hat.*